Yonder in the Sun

Poems

Daniel Fitzpatrick

En Route Books and Media, LLC
Saint Louis, MO

Make the time

En Route Books and Media, LLC
5705 Rhodes Avenue
St. Louis, MO 63109

Contact us at **contact@enroutebooksandmedia.com**

Cover Credit: Grace Fitzpatrick

Copyright 2023 Daniel Fitzpatrick

ISBN-13: 979-8-88870-132-4
Library of Congress Control Number: 2024931105

All rights reserved. No part of this book may be reproduced, stored in a retrieval system, or transmitted in any form, or by any means, electronic, mechanical, photocopying, or otherwise, without the prior written permission of the author.

Get you all three into the boxtree. Malvolio's coming down this walk. He has been yonder i' the sun practicing behavior to his own shadow this half hour. Observe him, for the love of mockery, for I know this letter will make a contemplative idiot of him.

—Twelfth Night, II.5

For Grace, Therese, Gabriel, Maeve, and Peter

Acknowledgments

Gratitude is due to the editors of the following journals and anthologies in which these poems first appeared.

- *Evening Street Review*: "The Student Recalls the Philosopher"
- *By & By*: "Estate"
- *The Sheepshead Review*: "Should You Ever Hunt the Woods Around Your Home"
- *Joie de Vivre*: "Poem for My Children"
- *The Crow of Minerva*: "Falcon," "The Bear"
- *Halfway Down the Stairs*: "Toward the Vanishing Point"
- *Dappled Things*: "Eccentrics," "St. Mary of the Stair"
- *Ocean State Review*: "The Mariner Goes Below to Sleep"
- *Panoply*: "Jubilee"
- *Thimble Lit Mag*: "Gibeon"
- *The Adirondack Review*: "Fish Market"
- *Scarlet Leaf Review*: "Picturing"
- *Poetica*: "The Carpenter"
- *Embers Igniting*: "It May Be"

Contents

Acknowledgments v

Contents vii

The Bright Silent Instant 1

Magi 3

I. Letters to the Dead and Other Obligations 7
    A Birthday for Maeve 9
    Before Mourning 12
    The Student Recalls the Philosopher 14
    On a Photo of My Mother Holding Me as a Baby 16
    Sloth in the Sunken Gardens 18
    The Lunch Hour at Mazzaro's 20
    Lines After an Interview with Allen Ginsberg 22
    Vision of an Urn 23
    for Priss 23
    Burning 24
    Estate 25
    Should You Ever Hunt the Woods Around Your Home 26
    Transfigured 28
    Poem for My Children 30
    For You, for Then 31

II. The Mouse Prince 33
    Falcon 35
    The Bear 36
    Odysseus and the Squid 38

Yonder in the Sun: Poems

The Vultures and the Owl at the Death of Hector 39
Plato, I Believe 41
Toward the Vanishing Point 42
Fantasia for Dawn 43
The Shield of Achilles 44
Plague Journal 46
Eccentrics 48
The Mariner Goes Below To Sleep 49
St. Mary of the Stair 50
Mary Jane's Birthday 51
Tongues 52
Arabesque on an Unfallen World 53
Blood and Bone 54
Ice Hole 55
Shakespeare in the Conch Republic 56

III. Alice, the Egg, and the Eye 57
   First Intuition of a Nuclear Mystic on Visiting the Pictures
      of the divine Salvador Dali 59
   The Second Self 61
   For Gabriel, Born Where Priss Has Died 62
   The Trouble with Names 63
   Jubilee 65
   Festival in Cadaques Before the Wars 66
   Lydia 68
   Gibeon 70
   A Disappointed Bridge 71
   Columbus in Wonderland 73
   Fish Market 75
   Dame Blanche at the Soup Kitchen 77
   Strandings 80
   Relations 81

Riding Death in My Sleep 84
Picturing My Friend the Philosophy Major as a Captain in
    the Army 85
Basil the Bulgar Slayer 86
Canal Street with Nuns 87
Still Life 89
Gabriel's Oboe 90
Lament for the Men Like Jewels in the Trees 91
Cain 92
The Carpenter 93
It may be 94
The God of Swans 95

Yonder in the Sun: Poems

THE BRIGHT SILENT INSTANT

While the making of poetry demands its hours of vision and revision, of struggle over the right word, of inner agony as to the question of whether the thing is at last, after weeks or even years of turning and returning to smooth a phrase, complete, the poetic impulse itself comes down in most cases—at least for me—to a single moment of attention. In these moments when poetry begins, a word or a phrase, an image or a metaphor, arrives like a snatch of music woven through the fabric of reality from the symphonic source of all being. Poetry arises from the experience of hearing at last what has been there all along and the urgent desire to erect the ecstatic moment as a signpost, as an altar, as an answer to the advancing specter of death. The making of the poem, the long act of altering, trying, and refining, is the attempt to turn the recalcitrant, intractable words themselves into the ethereal stuff of the original vision. Craft closes the gap between the beauty that in the bright silent instant illuminates the soul and the purblind, mewling thing that first appears upon the page. Only the best of poets in their best moments can narrow the gap sufficiently that the Word, the heart of poetry, shines through to the reader, drawing him or her into communion with the poet and the Word.

The poems here collected mark some ten years' attempt to cultivate, in broken bouts, the sort of attitude that opens the ear to the poetic impulse, that lets the world become the weave of sign and symbol inherent in it as locus of intention, of gift, of love. They are poems brought about by births and deaths and by the mystery of sin we navigate between. They are poems conscious of themselves as akin on some level to Malvolio's yellow-stockinged, cross-gartered behaviors he practices to his shadow. Poetry may in many instances be little better than the act Malvolio adopts at the rumor of a love heretofore unimaginable. And yet it may be hoped that the act of poetry should save us from becoming so many Malvolios—so many ill-wishers whose very smiling has become the object of mockery.

For all the hope of getting a poem "right," of giving oneself sufficiently to the art to do justice to the world that impels it, it is in the end enough to know the poetic moment, to feel the sudden charge of being that tells us of the passage of the Word. Perhaps in what follows, in the images drawn from the woods of Arkansas and the streets of New Orleans, from warm winter nights in Key West and days of sun in the hollows of Greece, from hospital rooms and altars and dreams, there will be hints of such a passage.

Daniel Fitzpatrick
New Orleans, Louisiana
March 2024

MAGI

There are no roads that lead toward
the star that has emerged to warn you.
There are no inns along the way,
no travelers to parse the dusty miles out
with stories of their own exotic countries.
There are no clustered palms, no turnings
of the path upon the sudden wonder
of a snow-capped peak, no lakes
to lap at the edge of your weariness.
This is the country of your unbelief,
throbbing with the million lights
your ragged wings have shadowed.
Now you are alone and on foot
in the coldest reaches of your universe,
when there at the beginning,
the place you scarcely trust
you ever could have been,
this cold flame has called you.
At first the going's easy,
once you've gnawed to the marrow
your grief over all these ages lost.
Time will melt into a single undistended memory
as you come upon the countless things
you loved to love
and find that now you love them more,

and the more is your unmaking.
For now you cannot touch them.
For now you are the ghost
in the shadowland of your seeming.
But the star burns deeper,
consuming your unquiet years
until you stand on the high bank of a river.
In the fury of the light the current
is a flood of loves, all the race of beauty
folded in the cold repose of death.
And though you can't keep down your horror
there is nothing left but to wade, to swim,
to taste the salt palmfuls the passing things
press to your lips and hear the cold cacophony
of slapping hands and groans and beating wings.
Though even as the first drops
slither at the back of your tongue, your shivering
grows still. You are drawn on in solitary warmth
till standing naked on the reed-crowned shore,
you turn to find the blackness you've passed through
aflame with what you thought had passed away:
friends, lands, beloved cities with their spires,
every lip and petal, each lash and bud,
striking fire from the unbegotten light
that up till now has blinded you.
Now you see the river that you thought was death
is a rose like an ocean, awash with angels

sweeping its crimson ridges, dropping grace
like grains of pollen in the terrible speed of their flight.
Nothing lies between you and the star
of your transfiguration, a woman with a child
in her lap, though even as you gaze
upon this secret in the recess of your soul,
the child seems to leave itself behind.
The tender arms extend and swell.
The smooth skin bruises, bunches up
with corded workman's muscles fallen limp.
The softness of the hands and feet is caked
with dirt, the palms and soles tortured into bloom.
You cannot see the blade that struck eternity
from blood but in this piercing you feel
all the weight of darkness into which you'd gone.
You lean to press the oozing side that is
your own great emptiness and find
the infant has appeared again to grip your finger.
And his touch is death to you,
and his mother's smile shakes you,
as if the universe were trembling
with the love that is at last your undoing.

I.

LETTERS TO THE DEAD AND OTHER OBLIGATIONS

A Birthday for Maeve

As we split the ancient riverbed
that sleeps between the road
and your grandfather's house,
a deer formed in the mist and hung—
as if forever—over stones
who've never felt the urge of current.

We left your brother, your sister
to play in the sun on the hillside.
Memories of rivers rushed
over rocks spotted with fossil rain
in the creek bed below.

Something older than the deer
seemed to sew itself of the fog.
It skirted the trailing hem
of the night. It pressed the ribs
of the Herefords that turned
white faces from the fog.

The mountains leaned over
the smoking golden bowl
of our city toward our windows,
toward the red trickle that ran
before you, the clotted flood
that followed. The mountains
are rooted in blood.

I'd forgotten so much life
was in the body, enough
to pool beneath the bed
and trickle still as you nursed.
The knuckles of my left hand have
split, and dark seeds squeeze
from Greek crosses cracked
into my ring finger.

The flow of blood has dried.
Someone has washed the blood
from your hair, and you are sleeping.
The blood beneath the bed has spread
and dried in the dark.

Your brother and sister are sleeping
on the hilltop. The creek is drying,
and the spring peepers are quiet.

The mountains have withdrawn.
Smoke is gathering in their pines
as image conjures image, veiling
itself with whatever is,
with whatever there is.
The mountains have grown old,
swelling toward the east.
Older are the fossil drops of rain
and oldest are the words
below the river beds and the roots
of mountains tinged with blood.

The dark has turned
its face away for now.
That faltering thought in the fog
still haunts us like an unremembered dream.

My knuckles are split like stream beds.
Your face is creased below the eyes
and around the mouth.
You are one of the words
spoken when the one beyond
our imagining bent
to mold his image in the riverside.

You are painted on the heart
of the world, the bow bent back
to flood the world again
with water and with blood.

BEFORE MOURNING

In the evening when the sun hung low
like ripest fruit and its light
bronzed the ribbons of sea
between sand bars,
we came up from the beach
and took you by the hands
and led you to the water.

The breeze was down. While we children
ran the soft cool backs of the bars,
the brown bay played around your ankles
and you squinted a little
as if the sun beyond the horizon
and the mullet leaping in the channel
and the frolicking embodiment of your love
were all too much, too mad, too intimate
to make a dusk for all the world.

In the morning when the sea was full
you slept. The rest of us sipped coffee
in the rocking chairs and watched
the fishermen drift to shore
ahead of the heat.
Primroses folded, and gulls
cried for the coming of the breeze.

And after tea and sandwiches
and talk of what would surely be,
you settled on the porch to watch
in wonder as the breeze came up
at two o'clock, exactly as you'd said.

And this was your endurance,
that as the world grew older
the things that made each day the same
were better than they'd been the day before,
that as night fell on your century
the words we spoke at your bedside
could lift your eyes
as if we had discovered
what we'd said so many times.

THE STUDENT RECALLS THE PHILOSOPHER

In the curve of a park in Irving, I lust
for the shock of canvasbacks so soon.
I imagine them as he showed me,
under mesquite's knuckles clutching summer.

In the curve of a park in Irving—a suburb
of Dallas, which is bleeding westward
beneath the banner of his holiness Pope Cuban—
three bronze children are playing in a ring.

On the third floor of the college on the hill
in Irving, he has turned from the bust of Hegel
and the ridges of Aegean seashells to watch
for the migration of pelicans.

In town down the monorail are caverns of masters,
white walls of museums rising through cypresses.
Sculptors' placards damn the Bank of America
and its green light smiling on the desert

which sprinklers have whirred into Irving.
Once in the park down the hill in Irving
he answered "bufflehead" as I pointed.
And the word porpoised on the surface

of my mind. The word pressed into my mind
and rose like a duck. My mind rolled like water on
the whiteness of its wings—the real duck's wings—
and spilled back into itself. Then, across Irving,

where MacArthur cuts the first of fifteen freeways,
his Audubon guide fell apart in his apartment
to the bufflehead, pictured with the other ducks.
And he told me of the coal mine Hitler had packed

with Michelangelos and dynamite.
He told me of stepping into sunlight
on the mountainside while the storks
clamored toward Egypt.

In a park in Irving—a city no one
has ever called beautiful—he showed me
the canvasbacks beneath the mesquite,
red heads rising again, again, birds.

On a Photo of My Mother Holding Me as a Baby

When I try to remember your smile,
I leaf through dinner parties,
commencements, chance meetings
with strangers whose names slipped
through my sweaty fingers.
All I can find is this picture.

There the light is dead upon us.
Your chin is tilted to my head.
Your hair shades your smile from
the sun heaving itself over the river
over the water where my eyes have wandered.
My eyes have rolled with my infant neck.

We were by the river, I imagine,
somewhere idlers still let beer dribble
through beards like Spanish moss.
I've seen them leaning on their bicycles.
I've heard them name the catfish
down in the dark, bearded with broken lines.

There your father hasn't died, and the blood
hasn't stuck in your brain,
and the miracle of your hands
springing back into Beethoven
has not yet happened. You can look
at Dad, holding the camera, and smile.

I remember nothing of that place,
though I remember running
over gleaming tiles into the dark
of your father's den, into his lap.
I remember the rush of his hands,
hard and smooth as magnolia leaves.

I remember the back seat of the car,
the burn of the buckle in the summer
and the sound of your voice filing your complaints
with those souls—us, your sons—strapped into the back seat.
By then you'd never have gone to the place
beside the river, that place I can't remember.

SLOTH IN THE SUNKEN GARDENS

In the amphitheater, painted brown,
my daughter calls from center stage
for me to dance to the Nutcracker.

I decline, holding her brother's hand,
trying to match his step despite
the syncopation of stand and stair.

We walk. Words whisper in the canopy.
They are hiding in the blooms
and in the race and linger of vines.

They drip from parrot-gnawed limbs.
At my feet king palm roots appear
like fingers from another dimension,

and for all the cling and brilliance
of the sun and the petals the sun has spread
like stars—for all the children's radiance—

now my mind is basking in accidie,
sick with Florida, sick with tourists,
sick with itself for sinking into memories

of Greece. My mind stalks the hollows
of Olympia. It runs through the crumbling
stadium and into mists of poppies, into groves

of dogwood and orange, freckled with dew.
It crouches in the golden gloom
of the long-gone temple of Zeus

and watches the shepherds in the rain,
the goatherds in the ancient rain,
choosing the kids for the slaughter.

We walk. I am sick with words,
sick with the sun because it's what it seems
to be, because the poppies tremble,

because the staghorn fern has fixed
itself to the live oak and someone
has staked their names into the ground

to lead us along, sparkling, into the jungle,
where a snake scribbles its way
across the path as my daughter points and smiles.

THE LUNCH HOUR AT MAZZARO'S

Across the table an Annunciation unfolds
as Grace tears focaccia for Gabriel.
His head is bobbing like a pigeon's as he stands
on the plastic chair, arms streaked with marker
and iridescent as the necks of pigeons.
She has just begun to show.

Beyond them a lady in hibiscus print
sweats over sesame tuna. Her fork halts
on the way to her mouth, and she draws a finger
across a white cloth, pecks a message
into the face of her phone, and wipes the screen.
In the sunlight beyond her, beyond

the patio, the palm fronds shiver. Their hiss
and rattle drowns in the swirl of ceiling fans.
One parts the lady's hair and she smiles and chews
as she meets my eye, and I turn to the green god
at my back. His neck upholds the clam
that crowns a dry and silent fountain.
The fans are like falling water.

At my back I hear Maderno's fountain
spitting its own applause on the stones
of St. Peter's square. Once I saw a seagull
stick its bill into the spout until it pulled
a drowned pigeon out and labored into the sun.

Yonder in the Sun: Poems

Gabriel will only eat the bread,
however many times he cried and said he wanted meat
while we squeezed through the crowd
at the silver counter and wandered past the cappuccino bar,
the wine grotto, the host of plaster saints
opposite the registers and bathroom doors.

As oil drips onto brown paper before me,
Gabriel spreads his pointillist meats—his salami,
his mortadella—and eats no more. At last
I set him on the ground and he leads the way,
just slow enough that the lady puts down her fork
and flicks a golden curl as he goes.

Lines After an Interview with Allen Ginsberg

Why is the lady beating her head against the wall?
Why is she beating her skull against the wall,
against the fluorescent light that hangs
like a sheet against the wall from her head
down to her feet? Why are her feet arched?
Why does she go on tiptoe to beat her head against the wall?
Are those her sons, the two small politely dressed boys
sitting in silence behind her? Are they not surprised?
Why are purple crescents shining beneath his eyes,
the one with hair like sunshine in the day's last cloud?
Has he been reading late at night?
Has he been hesitant to go to sleep?
Isn't he too old to smell of urine? Why was he lying
in the yellow damp of his urine on the floor
before the television while his mother tried and tried
and tried to tie her shoes to tiptoe to the wall
and beat it with her head?
Do they see the potted plant so patiently
reaching out to touch them on the shoulders
as they sit in silence and their mother beats
her skull against the furious white wall?
When will he stand and dragging his yellow odor
like the tail of an unnamed orchid take her hand
and untie her shoes and tuck her in to listen
with blood in her eyes, with blood straightening her hair,
as he recites a story he has read and read
while his hand lay at his side on the sheet,
unable to rise and turn off the light?

VISION OF AN URN
for Priss

That seventh month before we buried you,
while you waited on the desk in the billiard room,
you came to me one afternoon in a dream,
crossing the verge of the universe
where the Crucified awaited Satan
like a pirate hanged on the headland of being.

You stalked across the summer yard
through the long grass risen of the ashes.
All winter we'd been burning hickory leaves,
and the hot quartz now was nothing
to your horned feet. The deer looked up
from the bedded blades, but smelling nothing,

settled back into their flickering naps.
Between the rough-cut timbers of the porch
you paused and cocked a heron eye,
the silver divisible hairs swept back
as if in flight. There was nothing to say.
You simply stood, hunched like an urn,

and the black Grecian figures all along
your limbs showed the breath regressing,
consumed in the kiln. Once you'd asked us
to scatter you on the hill, never thinking
that we'd linger in the woods long after you could ask
if we'd heard the peepers singing in the creek.

BURNING

All October the tall grass
bent northward, uphill,
its ochreous pallor eliding the moonlight
as sun swelled and burst in the thinning oaks.

Then you walked through our Elysium,
your horned feet smoothed on the quartz,
and as you passed into a shadeless place,
the juncoes (snowbirds, you said)
scattered your ashes.

We'll spend the winter burning leaves,
raking black cautery across the packed hill.
Otherwise the grass will drown
and the deer will ghost to livelier woods.

ESTATE

Patrick is apportioning your estate
>*Cutting into your chest he found*

part of which lies in a white-handled knife
>*the emphysema far past hope,*

for prepping salad at Western Sizzlin.
>*the alveoli overblown*

You'd done it for walking around money,
>*like worn out waistbands*

the same kind you and Pat withdrew
>*from an older self, still changing.*

Saturdays after your hairdresser's appointment.
>*The bronchioles were breaking down,*

The envelope, by the end, held nine hundred dollars,
>*slicing your breath thin, thinner,*

and the knife blade, sharpened over thirty years,
>*less and less left for your blood,*

had thinned to a quarter of its width.
>*until the mask, working at last alone,*

I used it last week to slice a goat cheese quiche
>*breathed into your nose like wind in a cave.*

once I'd relaxed, finding you were not contagious.

SHOULD YOU EVER HUNT THE WOODS AROUND YOUR HOME

Should Patrick say he's seen
new shadows on the hill,
don't hesitate to crook your gun
and waste a while in the fog.

If perhaps your left sole's formed a corn,
try a counterclockwise hike
with stops to cock the jack pines an ear.
The mist will mute the leaves' alarm.

See how even spider webs are wet,
slung deep between the willows' bones.
Taste them: none will stick.
The silken cups are shining in the knuckled twigs
of dogwood. Creep close, blow, and watch
the vibrant limbs slip up a strand
and sip a silver drop in silence.

Peer up through the paltry nudes,
the hickories who've wrung
their hands too dry.

Shoot if you wish, or don't,
when the grey or red or white-nosed fur
starts to bark or savage a branch.
This is where they live as well.

Notice, though we've burned the brown litter
to the fire plane's half-excited circling,
we haven't spread your ash, or his.
Too often still we walk the woods.

Before you go, though, tell me,
did you ever see the nebulae
blooming on the bottoms
of the red oaks' darkening palms?

I saw them for the first today.

TRANSFIGURED

for Ben

It took your passing in the static of night
like a ripped sheet of stars for me to see them

come with Christ up the basking slope of pine,
never guessing what they'd beg the stones.

Were you still dreaming when the river ran
to ocean and revealed itself a rose,

prophets like a storm of scattered pollen
dazzling its flows of lips and petals?

Did the eyes that wouldn't see straight on
alight ecstatic on the shine that struck

those three beloved on the mountainside,
and did the low, rounded hunch of your back

soften at Love's last look, the sun's swift glance
outlasting every silence of the heart

to whisper that we need not speak of this
to anyone until today arrives?

Or will it take those resurrected wounds
to let us know that glint of mystery,

this gleam of God's image treasured in earth
since clay drew breath beside the dark water?

POEM FOR MY CHILDREN

The bar-headed goose that glances down at Everest
through the shivered pinions of the flock
strains itself no more than when the egg tooth,
the neck, the wet straw-feathered elbows
broke apart the shell in which the bird soul
burst from nothing into universe.

See the way so much of what we know
still quivers on the verge of itself:
the shell ginger clotted in its sheath,
the failing winter's velvet buds,
the frog egg jelly of the pond.

There is no anguish in the glory of a squirrel
all furred against the cold, forgetful
of its monumental horde, no labor
in the cunning of the crow.
Nature blazes in the ease of what is.

However she might prove her careless excellence,
you and I cannot assay ourselves.
The sum of our migration
stoops to glimpse the Himalayan peaks.
It shudders with what angels fail to fathom.
There is no easy end for us and yet is it
easier for the way light glances off a sparrow.

FOR YOU, FOR THEN

I can't remember what to say,
but I remember you,
the one who looked at me
until I couldn't hide,
until I didn't want to hide,
the one who watched
till everything I'd done was me
and still you let me see myself,
my doubled soul in the deep
where I'd dragged you,
down in the dark of your eyes.

I can't remember what I said
before I fell asleep and after
I said that I'd be coming home
but I remember running back
through the thickness of the morning
and I remember you.

I can't remember the rain's end
the day we learned what I had done,
but I remember the light in the upstairs window
among the naked branches of the trees
when the night had brought me home,
and I remember you.

I remember singing in the autumn sun,
my head in your lap in the moonlight
as the freeway went quiet and coyotes called,

the cold of your fingers on my scalp
as you taught me how to see the future.
I remember the redstart in the leaves
and how quickly you walked among the mesquites
and your green dress chill with Christmas lights.

I remember how we knelt
beside the bed
while the sun fell golden
the evening we were one.

I remember the sycamores, their odor in the rain.
I remember the close of the crowd in the metro
and how slowly you vanished in your blue coat
and the scent of your hair I carried
into the cold night of Paris.
I remember you.

I can't remember when I saw you first
but I remember you,
smiling at the top of the hill
below the oak trees,
the sunlight filling your hair
like flowing water.
And that is grace forever for me.

II.

THE MOUSE PRINCE

FALCON

For my daughter

Some sixty moons have crested since
your nails first gripped my shoulders.
Since then you've grown to know
the space between the morsel and my fingers
and to delight in clattering beyond my call,
the wheels whirling you farther and farther out to
turn and race back, not to my voice
but into the wind that made you spread
your palms and gasp before you could walk.
I've taken the threadbare hood,
like a soul worn down to its last body,
and set it, despite a decade's protests,
over the indelicate angle of your brows.
Without it now my eyes are sewn shut by the sun.

THE BEAR

You must know that the limbs rise higher
on the maple's northern side
and when the Fish would flicker
on your end of the horizon
if you wish to see the bear.

You must go past the last cut stump
to the lightning's final carving.
Rest your gun in the raw gash
and hang the compass and bottle
from the bark's charred tines

and stop beside the oxbow so
your face might be the fly
the brooding bass has never seen
and let it rise. Nothing itself will swell
in its rippleless disappearance.

After months hunting woods most
remote, you'll hear a neighbor's seen it
pawing the packed earth beneath
the feeder. Your brother, dropping by
between D.C. and Dallas, will snap

a photo up the road as he pulls in.
Keep on until its stench blinds you,
until it rises, daring your eyes to climb
to invisible stars simmering on its shoulder.
No one will know, and nothing will descend again.

ODYSSEUS AND THE SQUID

Something called it from the dark calm
where day is like an eyelid,
up from the ponderous cold
to spread itself upon the deep
like cloud along the night,
burning in the luxury of stars.

And the men with eyes like berries
in the tangles of their heads
cried the nightmare bird
fluttering in sun that plumbed
the cliff face grave with hawks.
The ephod head inflamed the wounds

sewn silent when the beaked ships
groaned from smoking Ilium.
Then the spears leapt up from lockers,
leapt up from hands into the choral
idyll of their anguish. And the cupped
arms curved against the skeletal bluffs,

languid, dignified, like pale limbs
lifted to the distaff. The war rhythm
drifted through the dream light
as irons sank into the shadow
like the soul of a murdered man
bending to drink a black lamb's blood.

THE VULTURES AND THE OWL
AT THE DEATH OF HECTOR

That's right,
with the rotten heel.
You've smelled it.

Thought he was dead
the way he played
that lyre.

But did you see
his mother? All white
staring at that shield?

Lord, yes, blood
in that. Daggers
in the dancers' belts.

Brought him to life.
Someone else'll play
that lyre now.

Who's this?
You up already,
crooked ears?

> Oh, move down, shit legs.
> No, no roost, no, not at noon even,
> not once the king came down
> and the monster let him into his tent.

Do you mean
we could have had
king today?

> I mean the moon was in his beard
> and he keened so the mice were still.

Soon, friend,
soon, yes, always
soon

PLATO, I BELIEVE

Plato, I believe, was ill
the day the Delian sails were furled
like jasmine in the full sun.

The gadfly's poems lay composed
as infants at the beaten breasts,
and myth alone could mediate the light.

Nerves verged on performance,
an Isthmian games before the newborn blind,
and the hummingbirds burned in the dogwood.

Then the weaver in his eighth new cloak
struck the strings and vanished through the harmonics
of old men half-dozing on the brief park benches

while the swans sang despite the cold,
sang still in spite of fear's far rumors,
rushing to the day beyond before.

TOWARD THE VANISHING POINT

The old dream freaks the mind from its music.
A lane divides the listening fields of corn.
A man walks. His shadow shows where sun splits
lindens. He saw them planted, saw the road
re-paved, saw the tear of artillery,
the rut and tramp of armor into wheat.
He saw the sprays of blood-bloom in the cows'
ribbed hulls, saw their necks dip, lips splay with froth.
His steps began in setting the saplings,
in seeing the round little root graves dug
by men whose faces flickered out of shape.
It was his animal soul that fluttered
in his throat at the half-empty table.
His shadow stoops where light divides the trees
while crows flow over the corn toward the night.

FANTASIA FOR DAWN

Since his is the pallor of the morning,
the king comes among roses, rises, sets
himself sentence: let let be last of be.
Lazes, sues for dawn's dawdling, descendant
of zenith, unmoved of mewling in keys
canted sinward. She suns, wails at thorn-thread
step to step disheveling, singeing, sung.

Then when the minstrels crow casements, climb, crowd
shepherds out of dew sips, flutes up meadows,
force flocks to lip crag-bloom and the cold cleft,
then same sun selves, assembles days of cloud.
She is. The moon is made. His hair lies lank
with water spun from Saturn and scattered
open-palmed along the furrows of world.

THE SHIELD OF ACHILLES

Go back to those songs
your careless strength sang itself.
Turn back to that attunement
of string and handmaid time.

Before this beaten scene
outstripping all our art
descended like a lusting oracle
to spread its ways, its histories,

its question wove itself
of lyre notes, of tides
lapping at the prow-cut shore
where you sat soothing yourself.

None who've known you, not you,
not the girl who made you
make yourself a curse, not
the classes nodding in the breech

of your rage—what countless
apocalypses since?—
would not have known the one hand,
the heaven of your vengeance.

Then the second hand rippled,
and the cloaks of the dancers
fluttered over daggers.
The cities you had dreamed

bled pale in their wedding,
in the promise of despair
that let the king into your tent
to see Hector—his Hector—accomplished.

Plague Journal

Meditations on the Seventh Seal

It is not the owl's cry but its quiet
that concerns us. Even the trees are still,
knowing the one who spread the devil's thighs
comes creaking, crossing rivers into their midst
to burn before she bears a second calf's head.

The artisan on the scaffold with the jug
of grain has swallowed us, wandering in the nave,
in agony, his tortures and his boils
repulsing all resistance, graver than nakedness.
The one come plodding from Carmel

confesses himself to death beyond the wall,
continuing that thought that's followed us
like a juggler's songs and oozes now
through the grate. It is everywhere, hooded
and staring, flickering beneath the tavern stew

and carved into the handle of the rustic hammer.
It is the grease of chicken skin that slips
from the fingers of the smith's wife.
The rude lyre delights it, and it
cringes, blushing, when the parade

of those who've taken bracelets from the dead
scourge themselves into the square and interrupt
the tune to task the peasant with his idiot
grin and bulbous nose, as though he'd never
hung a rabbit's corpse above a pond.

We know we'll see no one when the third knock
falls, and that we'll dance in the scythe's
ecstatic file while the juggler and his wife
look on, singing to their silent child
as visions stalk the sickness from the land.

ECCENTRICS

The gyre widens as the worlds evolve,
spinning in an ultimate attraction
through the light of ancient constellations
whose intimacy time has long dissolved.

Some tilt in, Franciscan in honeymoon
snow, melting in the blush of balding Sun.
Others, as Ezra, run and, dying, run
and revel in the mutiny of June.

One tans and, tanning, darkens to the heart,
finding fire fusing life with delicate
death. Blackness blends with light and lightly wakes.
And he unceasing seeks the deep cold's swart
sanctum from the dark God's celibate threat:
June's eternal, perning, rippleless lake.

THE MARINER GOES BELOW TO SLEEP

A slice of moon appears. A man descends.
He bears his constellations to his berth.
There, unveiled, they wheel and drive the shadows
from his musings. He murmurs, tosses, mounts
by dream up prick on prick of starlight. Still
some sun must swim a million years before
it bleeds the lidded flicker of his eyes.
For half his life this man has fled the shore.
He trembles at the sight of distant palms
as though the coconuts were pirates' skulls.
His cloister is the sea, its suffering.
His peace gleams in the twilight, in the net
that trails behind the sun and draws the moon
to blur the burning shore of all we know.

ST. MARY OF THE STAIR

Her beauty breaks the wave of consciousness.
Sun in the window flames the olive core
to oiled sheen, the smooth Semitic mantle
blossoming over the virginal curve.

St. Elmo's fire stuns me in the stairwell
thus, killing me turning toward the door,
confiding in a love I can't confess
without Democritus' atomics.

The endless dead do not discriminate.
They form their fate in chosen feats of love,
urging voided vesicles' ecstasies
and the cumulate wings' kenotic shock.

Still sculpted eyes stare spiraling above.
The stars engraved upon her shoulders swerve
beyond the sway of superstitious sticks
twin visions view, involve, and animate.

The brown eyes oversee the Pleiades.
The brown hands lift the lightness of the Rock.

MARY JANE'S BIRTHDAY

I see her there, three states away,
sagging in her sofa's gentle jaws,
the big screen at the end of the room
competing in the gloom with the salt

light slapping off the pool,
massaging the ceiling's grey paint.
She sees them more these shorter weeks,
the Bali feathers of inflected sun.

The screen sustains its voice,
her eighty-year ears ripping rabbits
from reality to thump the time,
slap the white waves in place.

She doesn't see the dust
descending to her threshed black lashes,
sprinkling the baby grand,
its lid left up since Lydia's death.

The keys lead nowhere now.
The keys are locked,
laid away along her clavicle.

Her music's grown as hard as light
and silent as the mermaids' psalms
bubbling up somewhere unseen.

TONGUES

Back then we sang our being into one,
pitching our teeth to the music
they'd heard whispered in the stars.

Rose and fell like shorebirds
coursing into coast winds, eyes half-lidded
with laughter unraveling on the smooth stones

sucked from urchins' embraces,
offered on the altars of stuttering tongues.
Spin the marble on its pedestal

and score the symphony of Aphrodite,
of bodies of goddesses chiseled
out of powdered earth. Harmonize

your haunting with the tide
that throbs about the girdled world.
Speak yourself and taste at last
the long lost land you still call home.

ARABESQUE ON AN UNFALLEN WORLD

Through the window where I wash the dishes
while we roll away from the sun,
I watch the growth of the distant mountains,
the low ridge of ground-down Ouachitas
like old molars in a wound-up jaw.

Picture a world where simile is law
and a civil service test could end
in brushing, flossing, bleaching the mountains.
All landscapes there are white. White canvases echo
down museums where critics creep up on each other's taste.

Relish the tension of a rat trap set for Satan.
Except he slouches with his weightlessness
and spends his time tricking us into the cheese
so that da Vinci had to paint the Last Supper.
In that other world they'd let the colors fade.

In that other world da Vinci doesn't eat supper.
(I say doesn't because there he's still alive
and the Mona Lisa doesn't prove the categorical imperative.)
They may be creeping up on us now,
snickering, hoping to spring us unaware.

At least if I am at the center of the world
the suds should still spill down the sink
as my window stares on mirrored mountains
reaching for the trees in each other's cavities
as we slide down the sun's sisyphean gullet.

BLOOD AND BONE

We've beaten back our breath to blood and bone,
And all our longing leaves us at the shore
To milk an anguish from a stricken stone.

The Bruges bell wakes us with its morning moan
As dawn on high descends from door to door.
We've beaten out our breath in blood and bone.

I've killed and cut the chords that could atone
For all the light I've stolen in to store.
Where can we milk the blood from brazen stone?

Mars is in the moon; his shining iron
Throne spins grinning on the fisher king's moor.
Still Peter's pence will breathe its blood and bone.

The bread has bloomed; the altar cloth intones
Its call to marble beasts to turn the score:
Milk an anguish from this Umbrian stone.

The rhythm rises; now the grave has sown
A warning of the Eden unexplored.
We've beaten out our breath in blood and bone,
Now milk an anguish, if you can, from stone.

ICE HOLE

after Marsden Hartley

Has the day begun
    to give you back yourself
like the trees at the edge
of the frozen lake
    taking back their nakedness
as flame rains down the mountain
and the clouds burn purple
with the shame or the sweetness
    that could both be yours.
Now the labor at the still white
water's laid aside: those single
    shining blocks cut out to breathe
the deep darkness like a scream,
like a killer gone limp on his cross
    calling you to gaze upon yourself,
to fall against the cold black mirror
where the rainbow of your soul swims in silence
    like a fish, like a seer, its eyes
enormous and unmoved.

SHAKESPEARE IN THE CONCH REPUBLIC

Like devils into Eden come the cormorants, wings spread
upon the sun or folded to the depth of dead worlds

where boredom's hectic monuments claim
the gospel of the damned. No pelican can stoop so heavy to the run

of minted herring. The thought of this unstable stay therefore remains.
Dorado clouds I've conjured rise to winter's honeyed flight before the moon

to vanish, I imagine, on Havana's glow. The vultures roost along
the highway by Miami. Their shit-caked scales have cooled and mediate noon-

day memories of naked lizards hooded in flame and whipping yellow
tails across the station's landscape. Again child's chirping. Again the naked

drive down midnight coasts where two sit speaking alone. Their backs are shells
to what we do not know. So many bloom the naked trees

to boast their cold diminishment of sap. Far from carrion gyres
fall names from singing faces, though I have walked the banyan home beside the sea.

III.

ALICE, THE EGG, AND THE EYE

FIRST INTUITION OF A NUCLEAR MYSTIC ON VISITING THE PICTURES OF THE DIVINE SALVADOR DALI

All rot. Sacs d'objet. Fifth avenue.
No more than manikin.
Cut it open. I'll find you some pumice.
Then again, whose blood?
That's what I thought.
I wash my hands 152 times a day.
Might as well split my mind.
They did already in a four hundred year daydream,
shut half in a machine man, said suck it up,
wound me, let me go, said not
to gasp at the piercing sweetness
of four pound monofilament
notching the split-lipped gash of finger skin
when the cichlid flips flaming on the deck.
How you gonna bring that in
bout the barley, fish?
Alice grew, got put up on a pedestal,
spilt milk on a pair of penny loafers in the desert.
Thieves, thieves, every which way, baby, oh.
Don Quixote de la mantra, de la Cointreau,
with the bull's balls quick to a windmill,
laughing his black and white head off.
Aquatint. Anybody heard a good joke,
had a dream the past few years?
All greens yellow in the sun.
Nature's last. Hardest to let go.
Age old butter dusk and
can anyone alive explain to me

the esse of pulchritude?
South Platte, elk in distance.
Unsung thunder up above the Divide.
Come out the salt breeze now
and we'll doze in the crape myrtle glade,
telling each other stories.
There goes gorgeous now
on the waves of the unripe world.
Let's unforget it finally in the moon vine.

THE SECOND SELF

You must come close before your soul
swims into view at the bottom of the doubled world.
That second self will float on eyes like altars
curved as gently as the earth
to give you back this you
which is not you, mirrored and multiplied.
The rainfall prays to stop and let you
scan the crystal deep of every drop.
The fountain showers you in you,
its million minutes scattering
your image on the stones.
The faint applause of it fades
with the antiphon of your footfalls
down the ancient sun-strewn street.
Know that I will never mind your seeing
no, not me, but the image of me like a mirror
melting on the surface of the unmoved ocean.
This is where all hope has left me,
abandoned to a mercy only opened when you turned
and offered me at last myself.

For Gabriel, Born Where Priss Has Died

Doors down from where she passed
while we blinked out on mountains,
he stooped into hysteric void
and lodged a moment on the universe's verge,
caped in a verb too great for us to be.

Not his the sudden sepal bloom
of Love shucked up along the beach
to burst complete upon the page.

The same white that mined
your suffocating skin
veined the purple feet
rooted from his mother's ribs.
The same strata broke along his brow,
as if he is to show me what has been,
like the star we know
millennia beyond the one we've seen.

THE TROUBLE WITH NAMES

Have you read the sun
that penetrates the universe
in the back of your hand,
seen these days how strange that is,
torturing fantasias from the brown
and slender neck
of the guitar?
Have your car keys and your wallet
appeared in the dish below the mirror
like a dead man's?

The twittering syllables have fallen
from the unfamiliar flowers.
Names like rinds lie forgotten
as the birthed world rushes up:
nudes foreshortened,
foaming from the sea,
the corner of a table
Gentileschi left to thwart
us into seeing.

Return to yourself
and watch the names snap
back upon the things
you'd left a moment
unremembered. Is it possible
these blossoms are
azaleas? That those
astonishing wings

could answer
to the small sound
sparrow?

JUBILEE

For us it begins in gulls,
wings weaving in place
in smooth muscular strokes
like gondoliers keeping their easy balance.
Now they're jockeying,
jostling each other to be
the white, unconsuming flames
atop the salt brown candles of the pilings.

The dawn of June hangs
still, breathless since
the wind went down around four
when storms stumbled past in the north.

Fingerling sea trout flood
the simple water's edge,
beating at the beach
like a litter at an endless sow.
The blue crabs crowd
the ribs of golden sand
where flounder like starred slabs
of seafloor slip toward land in silence.

Laughter flares, blackens in the broken Sun,
smashes through the image of itself
slicing from the deep to meet
the molten mirror that unmakes us.

FESTIVAL IN CADAQUES BEFORE THE WARS

Far out to sea it is still the afternoon.
In a lone boat, oars lost, there is no water left
nor strength to wave, to hail, to snatch at idle tropic fish.
None to swat the frigate bird's eye.
Peace lies thick as sunlight. Hours of light to go,
while here on our coast, in Cadaques, is it
too late to spy the night's reticulation
on the deadening waves, to watch it take win-
dows, rooftops, spires and vanes gone quiet at sight
of Orion whirling murderous from the
deep. Is it time to go and watch the fireworks
through the arches of the plaza. Will they gasp.
Perhaps I'll cut the fray from the line and tie
the hook again and try for sea bream below
the bridge. It's the time of year, and shall I watch
as mother jigs the knife—I will have brained it
against a rock—along its spine and turns and
holds its whiteness to my eyes. There, it is gone.

No prayer but the ship's ribs like hands
sprouting from the parched mosaic earth.
They are joined at the base of the palm
while the tortured fingers rise baked in place
insisting we must walk in sunshine, walk in
sunshine. Walt Whitman is watching the sea
that sends its boats to the edges of everything.
Wherever we look they appear just where
a fisherman has left them for the evening,
carrying his tackle home to wash

with freshwater and to eat a yellow bowl
of rice with lemon to suck the lemon
and watch the ants pool in the husk.

LYDIA

When you died
your mother sagged in her recliner,
stared three days into nothing
on the blank face where the world
had shown itself till now.

What was there we didn't say
those three deaf stuttering days
when you had died
and the clock refused to—

This is to say
that yours was not the death
that leers once more around the room and disappears
so that the world is left to shake its head
muttering never mind.

For we cannot forget
that final four o'clock you spent
suspended in your purple gown
between the grand piano and the stairs,
the way your comatose mouth turned down
as though you'd made your bed
about your soul,
simplifying
as water on a windless day,
while we are left endless,
trout drawn gasping onto sand,
scales sticking on skin

and tails waving absent and
refractory
        in the stream.

You are glad to have left us in awe,
and though the current eased our breathing,
we are still, sometimes,
alone and transfigured.

GIBEON

That forty-first year we too became strangers:
Shook off our stone homes, tattered our robes,
Shucked the crumbling bread from molded cupboards.

Mere miles out we met, shared tangled stares.
Our skin had never known the Nile.
Our sweat had never darkened Jordan's bed.

And in their wake we washed up on the ruins,
Gazed in their eyes on perfect excavations
Spared the ban on sworn deceit.

The pails have worn their paths astride my thigh.
The quail dogs prime their muzzles in my skirt
As I pass uphill beneath the yoke of noon,
Uncertain of this second birth.

A Disappointed Bridge

A hot voyage, then, even at night,
even when the storms sailed in
between the stars and their reflections,
impossibly distorted by the fevered sea.
So hot, so hard to say that we were anywhere
except when lightning paled the mountains
kneeling down the coast. The big ship
pitched. All day they begged us not
to go on deck. At night they barred the doors,
but we slipped out, the only two not sick, it seemed,
with a bottle brought that afternoon
by footmen, the bottle iced
in the single silver bucket on their
cart, sliding wall to wall.

We slid between the railing and the wall
and watched the mountains cower to port
and shouted unspeakable thoughts through
the storm's breath like a shucking knife between us.

You wept the jacarandas in that wind,
the long blue trembling spines tossed together
in the hills while the ocean heaved the beach
like a litter of piglets raging at a sow
troubled, almost, with their hunger.
And now the mere appearance of that word,
so useful in a song, swells your blue impetuous
memory, blue below blue in the glow of the cabin clock,
still spilling from beneath the face you'd turned

down upon the bedside table.

And swells your weeping for the flowers,
blue-against-sky swept down in shreds,
your weeping for the bees in the honey-dry hive,
wondering a moment in the sun and sailing off,
useless to the green denuded fronds.

Even you were sick that last night.
I heard you vomit in the blind brilliance
of the closet bathroom as I fell asleep.

Yonder in the Sun: Poems

COLUMBUS IN WONDERLAND

Death is reading letters in the corner.
His face is brown like a scarecrow's,
two summers too ripe, and his back
is shelled down over his lap. His leg
is crossed, ankle to the opposite knee,
and the read love letters from time
are heaped half open on the ground
like clam shells come loose in the sun.
Sleep is looking on like a crab
with its claw draped over a turtle's neck.
For 7415 years the dragon and George
have been at it on the sand
at the center of things. George has
always already won and daily
the snake finds a new gem
of a mouth and these letters
keep piling up and overhead
as if in another dimension
rooted in that shining sable flourish
on a lip—Its twirled ends twitch in sleep
with every second breath—Alice is
all grown up on top of a column.
Her breasts are huge with pictured children.
She is holding them, imagining them,
and her milk streams the way fish spit
bugs from stooping limbs.
Ants are in her milk, which pools
in a pair and a half of oxfords
forgotten in this desert.

Right this way around the back
of Christopher Columbus, landed
only moments ago, with flags snapping
and priests kneeling faceless in their hoods
and monstrous coral on the shore.
Right this way to the white room.
Look, there are airplanes landing,
airplanes lifting off and the rich in shorts
rejoicing on tilted decks far out to sea.
Look and hear a line of America's anthology
and rest in the jagged mouth of boredom
and relax, waiting for the dead to end.

FISH MARKET

If morning's fingers, massaging the cloister's walls
and modeled on the tingling of the blue canal below,
should wake you sooner than the cries of the nearest gondo-
 lier,
recall the guidebook's sixteenth bullet point
and take the still serene Rialto to the market.
Observe to your ambivalent companion,
if only to remind yourself, that there are contests
even Buonarotti couldn't win, scale models
sent in blind and cast upon the trash heap of the Masters.
Listen for the liquid tick the clock tower's
stenciled, fin-curved arms suggest. By then the flowers
may have brought to mind the quail dogs of Arizona,
nuzzling the towels that soak the hunters' thighs. Keep quiet.
Now you've come among the fruits. Darken a carton
with strawberries and sip one, but save the rest.
The herring have strewn the glistening ice with stars
and are commencing with their lecture on Clara Peeters.
There's your passage through Babette's Feast
and on to the Cajun tables that shaped your tongue.
The hermit crabs are clicking in their vat of steel,
veiling their faces in bubbles as if
attempting to ascend at least into the puncturing
Sun. Purchase one, without haggling, and with it
a fiddler, and tip them both back into the calm
colloidal sea, throbbing with engines. Even as the tang
of nets spread to the light reticulates the back
of your throat the two will have spun their tale
of the afterlife to schools infinitely more interested

than any you'll ever address. It is beginning
to be warm. Buy a bag of salted horse
as you return. No delicacy, it still with strawberries
can tell you more than Chesterton of pleasure.
The Sun's assaulting the Rialto, and a man
crouches, rolling green paint upon a worn wood panel,
continuing undisturbed as your head turns further and further,
knowing you will have to spend the rest of your life
trying to explain his importance.

DAME BLANCHE AT THE SOUP KITCHEN

Here comes Blanche
with polyester laurels
tying back her dreadlocked
such lovely hair,
here she comes
in off the edge of night
where John the Baptist hulks
beside the interstate,
weeds rooting up the bricks
around his rose window
as he cups a hand
to his marble mouth.

She drapes her woolen topcoat,
her leather, claims a chair,
leans beside the silver urn
of coffee while her shades
reflect exposed brick,
exposed duct, exposed pipe
shushing water over the heads
of men, yes, mostly men and mainly
black, scraping into places
at the red and white oilcloth.

You're looking I said
you're looking joyous
this morning says the man
turned toward her leaning
beneath the television

tuned to the cool front,
to the slaughter, to the mothers
staring into rear view mirrors
in case today the worst should come
though mostly what they watch
are eggs, sausage, vanishing,
the dark flood of coffee
receding as they speak
I was gay in second grade
but my dad I'm pissed off
hey hey blessed is blessed
somebody spilled here.

Yes, she says, looking joyous
in her lavender blouse, yes
sweet sweet sweet no cream
and thank you for filling it
and bears away the smoking
mirror shimmering with sugar

the Catholic Church, the Mormon Church
they say, their congregated stink
swelling the warm room like incense
like the uncured pelts of animals
till the call, Time to go, time to go,
I love y'all and it's time to go
Blessed is blessed they say
and God is good and Blanche stands
alone at last in the middle of the room
telling anyone who'll hear that God
is God, not good, just God.

Hear O Israel the Lord your God is
crouched against the wall,
waiting for morning to follow.

STRANDINGS

When the sun storms churn the northern lights,
the sperm whale spins his mad white belly
to the moon and spreads a cross against
the squid-concealing deep. This is how he sees
in stereo, with the ocean's night at his back.
Otherwise the world is split, divided by
the monstrous bluff between his eyes. Disturbances
a million miles distant wreck the iron
in their hides, beach them on the shore
of our horror. Dreaming steals away at that scent.
Those agonizing lungs concede the rainbow
of a morning torn from eyes become unshuttable.
Our paroxysmic local god is guiding giants
to the blind empyrean beyond the Dogger Bank,
where continental shelves upheave
the main of our uncertainty. This
is the foundering that wounds us.

Relations

Six times my bike was stolen
out of our back yard.
The fence, the chain, the bolt
made no difference,
our being home
or not being home.
Not just my bike:
dad's bike, mom's bike,
my brother's bike,
all their bikes, six times
over. A white caravan
stolen twice from underneath
our leprous streetlight.
And lawnmowers,
weed whackers
and the chain saw
dad swung enough Halloweens
that people crept up
peering into shadows saying
it's the chainsaw house
there's the chainsaw guy
and ran off laughing into the dark.

One bright winter day
I found myself in a McDonald's
across Lake Pontchartrain
in Covington, Covington of
the perfect white columns
on the perfect white porches behind

the perfect white picket fences,
Covington of the Tchefuncte
smooth tame unruffled river
with the plein air painter on the dock
and the cold bodies of the catfish
below, Covington of bourbon,
of heelers and pointers and spaniels,
of cigar smoke haloes
dogmatic mint juleps
and the stoical poet of the latter day malaise,
Covington.

The realtor's swept-back heron hair
shone at me across the table
as I ate a silent chicken nugget.

We stayed in the chainsaw house.
Bought new bikes, new mowers, built
new rooms upstairs when hurricanes
swept away the mortgage
with a chest of books
at my bedside. No more bikes
went missing,
though before a single
neighbor had returned
a brick came through
the window of the car.

My daughter's bike sparkles
on the porch of our apartment.
Its tassels catch the breeze

and give back every color
the sun splits into.
My children play with beans,
with the second bag of red beans,
the one that split somehow
between the Walmart shelf
and the rack in the pantry.

My parents have sold the house
and are moving to Covington.
My children sit on the floor
scooping beans in buckets of toy backhoes
and my daughter asks
when grandpa and nana will have
a new house and was it
a boy who stole my bike and why
did he steal it was he sad
did I cry what did I say to grandpa and nana
when I saw that my bike was stolen
and she looks through the window
behind her at the tassels rising like hairs
like fingers from the handlebars
and turns back to play singing
red and yellow black and white
they are precious in his sight
Jesus loves the little children of the world.

RIDING DEATH IN MY SLEEP

lines from Wangechi Mutu

In sleep I will slip down
and cheek the cool appeal of death.
It pricks me. Thumbs me up
into the bodiless un-sun.
The eye crack gasps and sweats,
sits up no, no, not yet come, subsides
against the stilling of the blood thump.
The smell of remembering,
no sweet rank and unbegetting flood,
no magic river of harmonized sighs.
I will await that drift of unthought
when the deep dismasts me,
thrusts up horn on horn of soul's end
to make me no man, heeled, crouched to
ponder eyeless, earless, conceive
somehow the once-was stripped, unlatticed
lying breathless in the earth
of moisture and love-root, rending mud
until the dust of woman
feels the sword tear there
between her perfect ribs.

PICTURING MY FRIEND THE PHILOSOPHY MAJOR AS A CAPTAIN IN THE ARMY

It's tricky to picture you
advancing your command across
Afghanistan's grey eyes,
the rough too-fluid tread
of turret, skirt, and coupola
through the documented occupation.

You resolve first that morning on the mall
a minute prior to epistemology
stepping in slow circles to crush
the night's weight of acorns
beneath your hard right sole.

And then through the dark
divided by the streetlights
shearing in between the blinds,
kneeling next to your bed,

and then, our eyes both closed,
repeating the officers' retreat
when the sergeant tore the goat's throat
out with a cheese knife
and looked at you across
the red right hand
fondling his scotch
and smiled.

BASIL THE BULGAR SLAYER

When they came, as he'd known they would,
into the canyon of yew,
he climbed a ridge to watch
the mathematics of his vengeance
applied. Where galaxies had been
a few moons flickered and smoked.
To twenty thousand legs a hundred eyes.
An eye to every hundredth man, precisely,
the columns ranged in sweet soft
teeming symmetries of pregnant spiders.
Lear-like their nightmare motion
clotted and oozed from the Aegean,
lids fluttering like shutters as the cranes'
familiar convoys sailed for Egypt.
A few were dreaming by the time they saw the tsar,
and like clockwork the blood clumped
in the narrows of his brain to leave him
two days' paralytic musing
while the blind like swallows
wove their indescribable way home.

CANAL STREET WITH NUNS

New Orleans, April 2019

The nuns (yes, nuns), are afloat on Canal Street,
shifting slipper to slipper, circling, making certain
their soles don't chew the blue-black

hems of their habits. Overhead in the broadway
of sky between the plastered store fronts,
the palms are draped with scents of jazz

guitars excavated from their cases. Streetcar
lines thrum their bull fiddle auditions. Across
the corner of Royal the man in the red hat

has rapped all morning for the tourists. A woman
turning toward work knows all his choruses
by heart and harmonizes as he smiles, slides

along beside her to the crosswalk, and skips
to his position as she slips into the Quarter.
The bell is clanging as the green car eases

to rest beside the abbess and her file,
coins in hand. They hoist themselves aboard
by brass fittings filmed with river fog

and fumbling palms. The wooden seats receive them,
spread them among laps glinting with lenses
and hard hands on sills, limp, sharing

their stigmata with the street. The broken
glide to the lake begins, and they flutter
past theaters and through the thundering legs

of the interstate and the cavern of oaks, road
caked in catkins. An hour to the end of the line.
St. Anthony's Carrara facade flickers in the leaves

as they disembark and cross themselves and vanish,
one by one, down streets of tombs resting
uneasily on moist earth. The shadows have gone,

and they feel their way by memory, glancing
now and then at a bronze stag upon a mound,
one hoof aloft, its verdigris gaze directed

the way they came.

STILL LIFE

In the midst of the gape of the red fish
to draw back, to take the half lemon left
in hand, rim lips to skin and work
flesh free, sour, with tongue and teeth
and set the whitened rind like a worn
breast beside the red plate and brush
a woman into place across a leafless bough.
She's taut as a water balloon above the knee,
where the what's gone out of her as though
a giant water bug, the one she kept
in the glowing tank beside her bed,
had taken her at the ankle and begun
to dissolve her. His beard is gummed
with yolk, and the pigments
are strewn about the house so that
the teddy bear's turned red and the drapes
are caked in yellow as if a large moth
had taken this time to flagellate itself.

GABRIEL'S OBOE

Compose yourself and admit your being.
Slowly the gloom that's kept you company
across the dusty sunlit plazas
and tantalizing ocean
and up the lightless thunder
of the waterfall will lift. Native radiance
will stitch itself of unfamiliar jungle
and hand you back your own amazement.
Only later will words curl through the undergrowth
and complicate the commerce of the soul.

LAMENT FOR THE MEN LIKE JEWELS IN THE TREES

lines on *Tree of Necklaces* by Jean-Michel Othoniel

What word can I hand back
to touch the tassels of your anguish?
My tradition is the morsel,
the cold tear like the drops that limp
the sparkling early iris.
Dip your hand into the dish with mine
and I will hand you over.
No. Will not Christ you.
Cannot claim what is is not
when I have not become it.
No more bite but murder
I'm afraid.
Can I give the rainbow
of the mallard's back,
the chill
that cuts my clothing
and the colorless shine
of needles in the wind?
Is there at last
the long-lost
of our oneness,
the rain trees'
throbbing husks
to score the intimated chorus
of the vein?
Look.
The light I could have treasured
strung forever in the moss.

CAIN

    first felt the slide of panic
as cornflame bit and drifted
off in smoke like something sick
slipping from the altar
of irredeemable stone. Never had
the sighs not risen, cringing now
at clodded feet like dogs
who've smelt the swelling of a hunger
older than their panting endurance.

Did God say
    you would die
        and did the smoke
refuse to rise
    and rake the hairs
        on Moses' neck as
flame leapt from the bush
    which burned
        and was not
            consumed

THE CARPENTER

For a moment he'd forgotten
the scent of drowning.
In the first grapes he'd forgotten,
though only for a moment,
the smell of cities flooded,
the bloat and bob, the rolling
gorge of the ravening fins.

No nails fixed human flesh,
shed any blood but his,
but starting when the weather slowed,
through cracks in the upper pitch
crept in the rot of sin
with the fizzing click of the crabs.

And on the mountain, maybe, guilt began,
burning savor gnawed the sweetness.

He often thought of forgetting,
and steadily forgetting grew
and dyed the ivory teeth.
And Ham, unexpected in the tent,
saw the salted nakedness
and watched the empty hammer hand
beating its barren entreaty.

It may be

           that when Adam saw
the first black storm in the East,
rigorous back unbowed,
rough hand resting on the rude plough,
his faith faltered
on the thought
that God had changed his mind,
sweeping up sheathed Eden,
letting Earth crack back to wordless void.

He and Eve died a skyless night
uncertain of another Sun,
trembling beneath fig skins and furs.

It may be, too,
that when the first Sun coppered the clay creek
and dripped behind the western wood,
no thought of its return
descended with the veil of stars
to the hushed bower and pillowed locks
and flowers
appealing to all but eyes.

Evening came, and night followed,
and the Sun amazed us with the morning.

THE GOD OF SWANS

Afloat on the sea of God
that is their souls,
they have no need
to waste a while dreaming
in the windows.

The rest of us,
drifting in the wake
of what we could be,
need moments, hours, days,
to turn away, to lay
the book down, dogeared
at the sentence we've read
twelve times, and wander
with the squirrel circling
its way up the cypress
or simply vanish
into the blue abyss
of wherever we are not.

The problem with windows is
you can't look through
the same one even once.
Every second that shadow of you
looms a little older in the glass
and the whole world has spun
to contemplate a different set of stars.

For instance.
Take a day at the museum.
Wander past Miro, Picasso, and Monet.
Spend three hours with the still lifes,
with the fish heaped on the shore,
with the half-peeled oranges
and rabbits hung by their hind legs to cure.
Read the artists' names a hundred times
and forget them the second you've left
the room. By now you're dazed,
no longer awed but overwhelmed,
almost, it seems, a little sick.

Here to save you
comes a window.

In the window is a swan,
sleeping on the still sea
of its own reflection
while the paddle boats
in the shapes of swans
churn the mirror
of the lake to mosaic.

For a moment you are the swan,
you are asleep in the safety of yourself.
You may at any moment
turn out to be a god.

But isn't it too much for us?
Can it be those sleeping wings
could spread, beat, rip
the shining water into rain?

Already this swan is too big to believe,
but look, it's growing every second.
Now you could ride it, slipping a thigh
behind each sun-drenched wing.
Still it grows, those awful feathers
flooding the shores of the lake,
stripping the palm trees,
urging all the smaller birds
to shriek the end of time.

And still it grows, tipping the museum on end,
shaking all the paintings from the walls,
shearing them forever from their makers.
When the god of swans has descended
once again into the realm of dreams,
no one will remember their names,
who imagined Cupid could have learned
love's fury in the face of his beautiful mother,
who told the lie of sunset on the bayou
when the light's just so and the snakes
have stayed away from Eden
and half a million mosquitoes aren't doubled
on the water's windless face.

Soon it will be night, and the swan will gleam
with the lamplight and the moon, and the walls
of the museum will gleam as well and in the dark,
by the red glow of the exit signs, the artists
will be dead another day, while the swan
will shift its neck and set its beak
afresh among the feathers, never quite asleep.

www.ingramcontent.com/pod-product-compliance
Lightning Source LLC
LaVergne TN
LVHW051845080426
835512LV00018B/3082